SET UP. SELL. STAND OUT.

A BOLD GUIDE TO PLANNING AND PROFITING FROM POP-UP EVENTS AND FESTIVALS

TAMEKA CREWS & JORDAN CREWS

Disclaimer - By reading this book and participating in pop-up shops and festivals, you acknowledge and understand that we are not responsible for any financial losses or damages that may occur. Your decision to participate is voluntary and based on your assessment of the risks and potential rewards.

Introduction:

Welcome to the ultimate guide on preparing for a successful Pop-Up Event or Festival! Our book covers everything you need to know, from answering all your questions about Pop-Up Events and Festivals to detailed preparation tips. We've even included a dedicated chapter with a handy checklist to ensure your events are flawlessly planned. Prepare to embark on a journey to a truly memorable Pop-Up Event or Festival experience!

Pop-Up Shops and Events

1. Definition and Purpose:

- **Pop-Up Shops:** Temporary retail spaces that allow businesses to engage directly with customers in high-traffic locations or events.

- **Pop-Up Events:** Temporary installations or experiences that create buzz and engagement around a brand, product, or cause.

Table of Contents

(Ms.Unexpected) Tameka

and

(DJ Mojo) Jordan Crews as Narrators

Chapter 1

"Picking and Planning Festivals, Pop-Ups and Events"

"Believe in yourself as passionately as you believe in your business. Your unwavering confidence is the cornerstone of every success story."

Ms. Unexpected

When selecting a festival and Pop-Up to participate in, several key factors come into play to ensure your experience is rewarding and successful. Understanding these considerations can help you strategically align your brand with the right audience and maximize your impact at the event.

1. Festival types:

- **Music Festivals:** These are centered around live music performances and often draw large crowds over several days.

- **Food Festivals:** Focus on culinary delights, offering opportunities for food vendors and culinary experiences.

- **Cultural Festivals:** Celebrate specific cultures, traditions, or holidays, offering a platform for diverse activities.

- **Art Festivals:** Showcase visual arts, crafts, and performances, appealing to artists and art enthusiasts.

- **Local/Community Festivals:** Held at the neighborhood or city level, emphasizing local businesses and community engagement.

Choosing the right festival involves carefully assessing your target audience, estimating foot traffic, evaluating costs versus potential returns, aligning with your brand values, and considering logistical factors. By taking these elements into account, you can make informed decisions that enhance your presence and engagement at the festival, ultimately contributing to the overall success of your participation.

2. Factors to Consider When Choosing a Festival:

- **Target Audience:** Match your product or service with the demographics of festival attendees.

- **Foot Traffic:** Estimate the number of attendees and their potential interest in your offerings.

- **Cost vs. Return on Invest (ROI):** Evaluate participation fees, setup costs, and potential revenue or exposure.

- **Brand Alignment:** Ensure the festival's values and atmosphere align with your brand identity.

- **Logistics:** Consider logistics such as location, accessibility, setup/breakdown times, and vendor amenities.

Carefully assessing foot traffic at a festival helps you gauge potential exposure and engagement opportunities for your brand. By participating in events with substantial attendance and interest in your offerings, you can maximize your visibility, attract more customers, and optimize your overall participation experience.

3. Steps to Participate in a Festival:

Participating in festivals presents a valuable opportunity for businesses to connect with new audiences, showcase their products or services, and build brand recognition. However, achieving success at these events requires careful planning and execution. Listed below is a guide to navigating the essential steps involved in participating in a festival, from initial research and selection to post-event follow-up.

- **Research and Selection:** Identify relevant festivals through online searches, industry associations, or local event listings.

- **Application Process:** Complete the vendor application, including details about your products and services, booth requirements, and insurance information.

- **Prepare for the Event:** Plan your booth setup, promotional materials, inventory, staffing, and payment systems.

- **On-site Execution:** Arrive early for setup, engage attendees effectively, and monitor sales and feedback.

- **Follow-Up:** Capture leads, gather feedback, and assess the event's impact on your business.

Successfully participating in a festival involves a strategic approach encompassing thorough research, meticulous preparation, effective on-site execution, and diligent follow-up. By investing time and effort into each step—from identifying suitable festivals to engaging attendees and evaluating outcomes—you can maximize the benefits of festival participation for your business. Whether it's enhancing visibility, generating leads, or strengthening customer relationships, each stage plays a crucial role in achieving your goals and ensuring a rewarding festival experience.

1. Planning a Pop-Up:

- **Goals and Objectives:** Define what you want to achieve, such as sales, brand awareness, or product launches.

- **Location:** Choose a venue with high foot traffic that aligns with your target audience.

- **Legal Considerations:** Obtain permits, insurance, and licenses required for the location and type of event.

- **Budgeting:** Calculate costs for rent, staffing, decor, inventory, marketing, and any special features or activities.

- **Marketing and Promotion:** Use social media, local advertising, and partnerships to promote your pop-up.

2. Executing a Successful Pop-Up:

- **Design and Layout:** Create an inviting space that reflects your brand identity and showcases your products effectively.

- **Customer Experience:** Offer unique experiences, exclusive products, or interactive elements to attract and engage visitors.

- **Staffing:** Train your team to provide excellent customer service and product knowledge.

- **Sales and Transactions:** Ensure smooth transactions with POS systems or mobile payment options.

- **Data Collection:** Capture customer information and feedback to build relationships and measure success.

3. Post-Pop-Up Evaluation:

- **Assess Results:** Review sales data, customer feedback, social media engagement, and media coverage.

- **Learn and Adapt:** Identify strengths and areas for improvement to enhance future pop-up strategies.

- **Follow-Up:** Continue engaging with attendees through email, social media, or promotions to maintain momentum.

4. Benefits of Pop-Ups:

- **Flexibility:** Test new markets, products, or concepts without long-term commitments.

- **Brand Awareness:** Increase visibility and attract new customers through direct interaction.

- **Community Engagement:** Connect with local communities and build relationships beyond online interactions.

- **Innovation and Creativity:** Showcase creativity and innovation in product presentation and customer experience.

Conclusion

Picking festivals and organizing pop-up shops and events can be valuable strategies for businesses to expand their reach, engage directly with customers, and build brand awareness. By carefully selecting the right festivals and planning engaging pop-ups, businesses can create memorable experiences that drive sales and foster customer loyalty. Evaluating performance and learning from each event helps refine strategies and maximize future opportunities in these dynamic marketing channels

Chapter 2

"Comprehensive Checklist: Ensuring Efficiency and Accuracy"

"Efficiency without accuracy is haste; accuracy without efficiency is delay. Strive for the delicate balance where both meet seamlessly for optimal results."

Ms. Unexpected

By following this checklist and preparing thoroughly, you will be well-equipped to handle various situations that may arise during festivals and pop-up shops, ensuring a successful and safe experience for both you and your customers.

1. Basic Supplies:

- **Tent/Booth Setup:**

  - Tent or booth structure (including stakes, weights, or tie-downs)

  - Table(s) and chairs

- ○ Tablecloths, covers, or displays

- ○ Signage (banner, posters, or signs with your brand/logo)

- ○ Lighting (battery-powered or generator if needed)

- ○ Rugs or mats

- **Tools and Equipment:**

  - ○ Multi-tool or Swiss army knife

  - ○ Duct tape, zip ties, extension cords, outlets, and rope (for quick repairs and securing items)

  - ○ Scissors and box cutter

  - ○ Pens, markers, and notepads

  - ○ Cart or totes for products or merchandise

  - ○ Solar-powered light or battery-operated light for inside/outside of the tent

- **Display and Merchandising:**

  - ○ Product inventory and display items (shelves, racks, hangers, etc.)

  - ○ Price tags, labels, and signage for products

  - ○ Display stands or easels for signage

  - ○ Merchandise bags or boxes for sales

  - ○ Samples ready for customers

2. Sales and Transactions:

- **Payment Systems:**

  - Cash box with change (coins and small bills)

  - Credit card reader and chargers (if using mobile or POS systems)

  - Receipts or invoice book

- **Security and Safety:**

  - Lockable cash box or safe for storing money

  - Personal identification and vendor permits/licenses

- **Taxes:**

  - ★ "If you pay taxes at a pop-up or event, remember to accurately record the tax amount for filing purposes. Keeping meticulous records ensures compliance and smooth tax reporting."

3. Health and First Aid:

- **First Aid Kit:**

  - Bandages (various sizes), adhesive tape, and gauze pads

  - Antiseptic wipes or spray

  - Pain relievers (e.g., acetaminophen or ibuprofen)

  - Tweezers, scissors, and disposable gloves

- ○ Cold packs and heat packs

- ○ Prescription medications (if applicable)

- **Personal Hygiene:**

  - ○ Hand sanitizer and hand wipes

  - ○ Tissues and paper towels

  - ○ Sunscreen and lip balm with SPF

  - ○ Insect repellent

  - ○ Personal medications and prescriptions

4. Weather Preparedness:

- **Clothing and Protective Gear:**

  - ○ Weather-appropriate clothing (rain gear, jackets, hats, etc.)

  - ○ Umbrellas or rain ponchos

  - ○ Sun hats, sunglasses, and comfortable shoes

- **Weather Monitoring:**

  - ○ Weather forecast updates (via smartphone apps or local news)

  - ○ Emergency shelter plan in case of severe weather (evacuation route, nearby shelters)

5. Communication and Documentation:

- **Event Documents:**

  - Vendor agreements and permits/licenses

  - Event schedule and booth assignment map

  - Contact list of nearby vendors and organizers

- **Communication Tools:**

  - Fully charged cell phone(s) with emergency numbers saved

  - Portable charger or power bank

  - Walkie-talkies or two-way radios (if communication with team members is necessary)

6. Food and Refreshments:

- **Snacks and Water:**

  - Non-perishable snacks (granola bars, nuts, dried fruit)

  - Bottled water or refillable water bottles

  - Disposable cups and napkins

7. Marketing and Promotion:

- **Promotional Materials:**

  - Business cards, flyers, and brochures

  - Promotional giveaways (branded items, samples, etc.)

- Email signup sheet or digital device for collecting customer information

8. Emergency Preparedness:

- **Emergency Kit:**

  - Flashlight or headlamp with extra batteries

  - Whistle or signal mirror

  - Emergency blanket or poncho

  - Personal ID and emergency contact information

- **Evacuation Plan:**

  - Familiarize yourself with the event venue's emergency exits and evacuation procedures.

  - Establish a meeting point outside the venue in case of evacuation.

9. Miscellaneous:

- **Trash Bags and Cleaning Supplies:**

  - Trash bags for waste disposal

  - Cleaning wipes or spray for maintaining cleanliness

- **Entertainment and Comfort:**

  - Portable seating or cushions for comfort during downtime

- ○ Reading materials or entertainment (books, magazines, games)

10. Additional Considerations:

- **Vendor-Specific Items:**

  - ○ Product-specific tools or accessories

  - ○ Extra packaging materials (bubble wrap, tissue paper, etc.)

- **Local Resources:**

  - ○ Know the location of nearby hospitals, pharmacies, and emergency services.

Tips for Packing and Preparation:

- **Start Early:** Begin packing well in advance to avoid last-minute stress and ensure you have everything you need.

- **Check and Double-Check:** Use this checklist to systematically go through each item, ensuring nothing important is overlooked.

- **Label and Organize:** Label boxes or bags clearly to locate items quickly when setting up or during emergencies.

- **Delegate Responsibilities:** If you have a team, assign specific tasks and responsibilities to streamline setup, sales, and emergency procedures.

- **Review and Update:** Periodically review and update your packing checklist based on feedback from previous events and changing needs.

Chapter 3

"Display & Social Media Advertisement – Selling the House"

"Sell your product like a house: highlight its best features and make it irresistible."

Dj Mojo

Preparing for a successful pop-up event requires a strategic blend of eye-catching displays, a unique presence that stands out from the crowd, and effective social media advertising. These elements work together to attract visitors, engage potential customers, spread the word about your brand & help you see what's comfortable for you in serving your customers. In this chapter, we'll delve into how to make the most of your pop-up displays, and tips for standing out and leveraging social media to maximize your event's reach.

Designing Effective Pop-Up Displays:

Understanding the Importance of Visual Appeal: Your display is often the first thing people notice at a pop-up event.

It's essential to make a strong visual impact to draw attendees in and encourage them to learn more about your products or services.

- **Color and Branding:** Use colors that align with your brand. Bright, bold colors can attract attention, but ensure they match your brand's identity. Having your Logo in as many suitable places as possible helps the customer remember your brand & for others to know who you are and what you stand for.

- **Clear Messaging:** Your display should convey your brand's message quickly and clearly. Use large, readable fonts and concise text.

- **High-Quality Graphics:** Invest in high-resolution images and professional graphics. Blurry or pixelated images can detract from your brand's perceived quality.

  - Interactive and Engaging Elements

  - Creating an interactive experience can significantly increase engagement and leave a lasting impression.

- **Product Demos/tutorials:** Live demonstrations allow visitors to see your product in action, providing a hands-on experience.

- **Catalog:** Catalogs with information about your products can engage visitors and provide additional information.

- **Photo Opportunities:** Create Instagram-worthy setups where visitors can take photos. This not only engages them but also encourages social sharing.

- **Strategic Layout and Design:** The layout of your display should facilitate easy navigation and highlight key products or information.

Open and Inviting: Avoid clutter. An open layout with clear paths makes it easier for people to enter and explore. There are different types of table layouts and here are just a few L-shaped, U-shaped, Z-shaped, V-shaped, Single table, and two tables shaped like an equal sign.

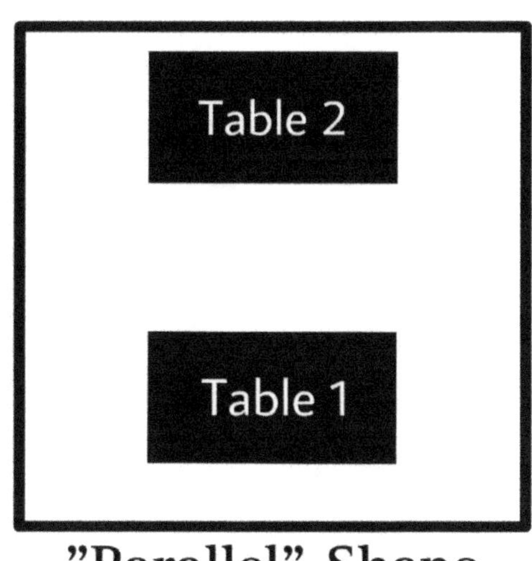

”Parallel” Shape

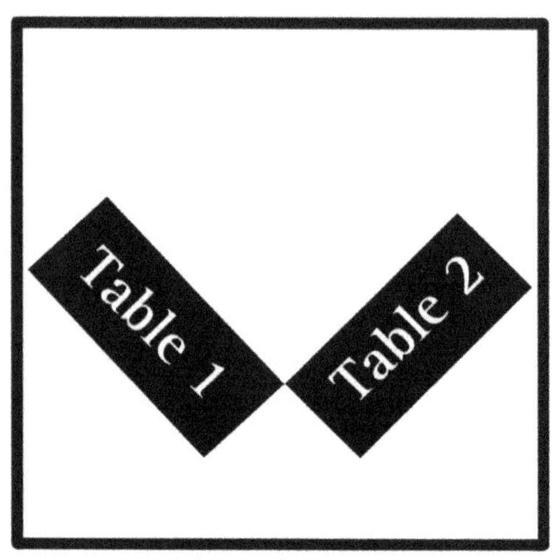

"V" Shape

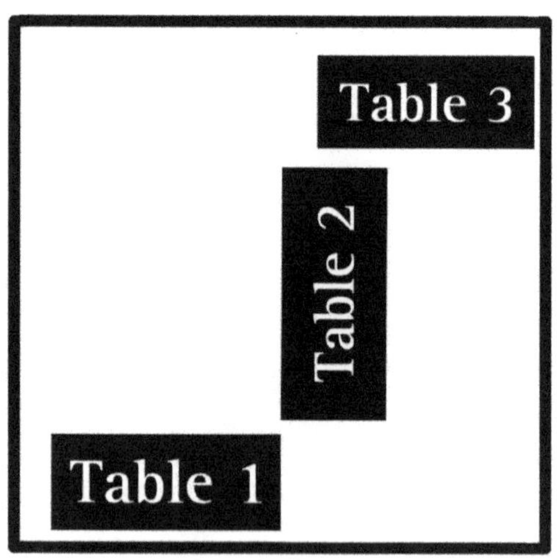

"Z" Shape

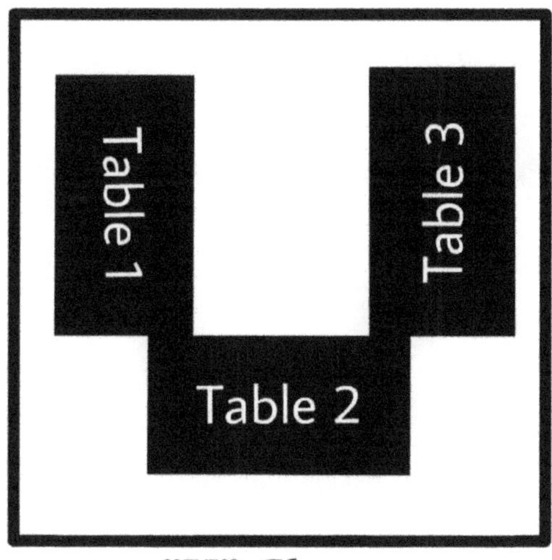

"U" Shape

"L" Shape

- **Highlight Key Products:** Position your best-selling or most attractive products at eye level where they are easily visible.

- **Comfortable Spaces:** Provide areas for visitors to sit or rest if possible. Comfortable visitors are more likely to spend time at your booth.

Standing Out at a Pop-Up Event

- **Unique Themes and Concepts:** Adopting a unique theme can set your pop-up apart from the competition and create a memorable experience.

- **Seasonal Themes:** Align your event with holidays or seasons. For example, a summer-themed event with beach decor can attract attention.

- **Storytelling:** Create a narrative around your brand or products. Tell a story through your displays and interactions.

- **Exclusive Offers:** Offer something unique that visitors can only get at the pop-up, such as limited-edition products or special discounts.

- **Engaging Activities:** Activities that engage visitors can increase dwell time and create a buzz around your pop-up.

- **Games and Contests:** Simple games or contests with prizes can attract and entertain visitors.

- **Personalized Interactions:** Personalized interactions can enhance visitor experience and build a connection with your brand.

- **Greeting and Assistance:** Have friendly staff ready to greet visitors and provide information.

- **Personalized Recommendations**: Use quizzes or surveys to offer personalized product recommendations.

- **Follow-Up Opportunities:** Collect visitor information to send follow-up emails or offers. Ensure this process is smooth and respectful of privacy.

Social Media Advertisement:

- **Pre-Event Teasers and Announcements:** Building anticipation before the event can increase attendance and engagement.

- **Countdown Post**: Create a countdown series on social media, highlighting what to expect each day leading up to the event.

- **Sneak Peeks**: Share sneak peeks of products, displays, or exclusive offers that will be available.

- **Event Details**: Regularly update followers with event details, including date, time, location, and any special activities.

- **Live Event Coverage:** Providing live coverage of your pop-up event on social media can engage your audience in real time and attract more visitors.

- **Live Streaming**: Use platforms like Instagram Live, Facebook Live, or TikTok to stream parts of the event, such as product demos or performances.

- **Real-Time Updates:** Post-real-time updates and stories showcasing different aspects of the event.

- **Engagement Prompts:** Encourage followers to interact with live content by asking questions, conducting polls, or running contests.

- **Post-Event Content:** Continuing to post content after the event can extend its impact and keep your audience engaged.

- **Event Recaps:** Share highlights and recaps of the event, including photos and videos of key moments.

- **Thank You Posts:** Thank attendees and participants, for showing appreciation for their support.

- **User-Generated Content:** Encourage attendees to share their own photos and experiences from the event, and repost this content on your channels.

- **Your Display Is an Image Itself:** Your display is not just a physical setup; it is a visual representation of your brand that can be shared widely on social media.

- ***Capturing the Perfect Shot:*** High-quality photos of your display can be powerful marketing tools.

- **Professional Photography**: Consider hiring a professional photographer to capture your display and event.

- **Variety of Angles**: Take photos from multiple angles to showcase different aspects of your display.

- **Focus on Details**: Highlight unique or intricate details of your setup that reflect your brand's personality.

- *Social Media Posts:* Use your display photos in social media posts to continue promoting your brand even after the event.

- **Behind-the-scenes**: Share behind-the-scenes photos of setting up the display to build excitement.

- **Highlight Products**: Post photos that highlight key products within your display.

- **Engagement Hashtags**: Use event-specific or brand-specific hashtags to increase the reach of your posts.

- ***Encouraging User-Generated Content:*** Encourage event attendees to take and share their own photos of your display.

- **Photo Contests:** Run a contest where attendees post their photos with a specific hashtag for a chance to win a prize.

- **Social Sharing Incentives**: Offer discounts or freebies to visitors who share photos of your display on social media.

- **Tagging and Mentions:** Encourage visitors to tag your brand in their posts, increasing your online visibility.

32

Conclusion

Combining visually appealing displays, unique and engaging elements, and strategic social media advertising can significantly enhance the success of your pop-up event. Remember, your display is an image itself, capable of drawing attention both in-person and online. By effectively leveraging these strategies, you can create a memorable experience that resonates with visitors and extends your brand's reach well beyond the event.

Chapter 4

Mannerisms: "Sell as If you are selling to yourself"

"Give what you want to Receive"

Dj Mojo

The success of a pop-up event hinges not only on the visual appeal of your displays and the quality of your products but also on the behavior and attitude of your staff. Mannerism , customer interactions, and overall atmosphere play a crucial role in creating a positive and memorable experience for visitors. This chapter will explore the significance of mannerisms during a pop-up event, the golden rule of treating people how you want to be treated, and the importance of having fun.

The Importance of Mannerisms at a Pop-Up Event

1. First Impressions Matter

The first impression a visitor gets when they approach your business can set the tone for their entire experience. Here are a few suggestions:

- **Friendly Greetings**: A warm and genuine greeting can make visitors feel welcome and valued. Smile, make eye contact, and offer a friendly hello.

- **Professional Appearance**: Ensure your staff is dressed appropriately and reflects the image of your brand. Clean, branded attire can enhance professionalism.

- **Positive Body Language**: Open body language, such as uncrossed arms and facing visitors directly, creates an inviting atmosphere.

2. Active Listening

Active listening is key to understanding and addressing visitors' needs effectively.

- **Show Interest**: Nod and make verbal acknowledgments to show you are engaged. Avoid interrupting while the visitor is speaking.

- **Ask Questions**: Ask open-ended questions to encourage visitors to share more about their needs and preferences.

- **Clarify and Confirm**: Repeat back key points to ensure you've understood correctly and confirm details with the visitor.

3. Knowledgeable Assistance

Being knowledgeable about your products and services can enhance the visitor experience.

- **Product Familiarity**: Ensure all staff members are well-versed in the features, benefits, and uses of your products.

- **Prompt Responses**: Respond to questions confidently and promptly. If you do not know the answer, find out or direct the visitor to someone who does.

- **Educational Interactions**: Educate visitors about your products in a way that is informative and engaging without being overly sales-focused.

4. Treating People How You Want to Be Treated

1. The Golden Rule in Customer Service

The principle of treating others as you want to be treated is foundational to excellent customer service.

- **Respect and Courtesy**: Show respect and courtesy to all visitors, regardless of their purchasing intent. This builds goodwill and a positive reputation.

- **Patience and Understanding**: Be patient with visitors, especially those who may need more time to make a decision or have numerous questions.

- **Empathy**: Try to understand things from the visitor's perspective. Empathy can guide you in providing the best possible service.

2. Building Relationships

Focusing on relationship-building rather than just sales can lead to long-term customer loyalty.

- **Personalized Interactions**: Personalize your interactions by remembering names and details about previous conversations when possible.

- **Follow-Up**: If a visitor expresses interest in something specific, follow up with additional information or a special offer after the event.

- **Sincere Gratitude**: Thank visitors for their time and interest, regardless of whether they make a purchase. Gratitude fosters positive feelings and lasting impressions.

3. Handling Difficult Situations

Occasionally, you may encounter challenging situations or unhappy visitors. Handling these with grace is crucial.

- **Stay Calm**: Keep a calm and composed demeanor, even if the visitor is upset or frustrated.

- **Listen and Validate**: Listen to the visitor's concerns without interrupting and validate their feelings. Acknowledge the issue and apologize if appropriate.

- **Seek Solutions**: Focus on finding a solution that satisfies the visitor. Offer alternatives or compromises when necessary.

Having Fun at a Pop-Up Event

1. Creating a Positive Atmosphere

A fun and positive atmosphere can enhance the overall experience for visitors and staff alike.

- **Energetic Environment**: Play upbeat music, and maintain an energetic and lively environment.

- **Friendly Competitions**: Engage visitors with friendly competitions or games that are related to your brand.

- **Interactive Elements**: Incorporate interactive elements that are enjoyable and engaging, such as contests or live demonstrations.

2. Encouraging Staff Enthusiasm

Happy and enthusiastic staff can significantly impact the visitor experience.

- **Team Spirit**: Encourage team spirit among staff members.

- **Positive Attitudes**: Promote positive attitudes by highlighting the fun aspects of the event and celebrating small successes.

- **Support and Encouragement**: Provide support and encouragement to staff, recognizing their hard work and contributions.

3. Engaging with Visitors

Engaging with visitors in a fun and lighthearted way can leave a lasting impression.

- **Conversational Tone**: Use a conversational tone rather than a formal or sales-heavy approach.

- **Humor and Warmth**: Appropriate humor and warmth can make interactions more enjoyable and memorable.

- **Interactive Questions**: Ask visitors engaging questions that relate to their interests and experiences.

2. Lessons Learned

Learning from both successes and challenges can improve future pop-up events.

- **Flexibility and Adaptability**: Be prepared to adapt to unexpected situations, such as weather changes or technical issues, while maintaining a positive attitude.

- **Continuous Improvement**: Gather feedback from visitors and staff after the event to identify areas for improvement and celebrate successes.

Lastly, mannerisms, the principle of treating others well, and having fun are crucial components of a successful pop-up event. By focusing on these elements, you can create a welcoming and engaging atmosphere that leaves a positive and lasting impression on visitors. Remember, a friendly smile, a helpful attitude, and a bit of fun can go a long way in making your pop-up event a memorable and enjoyable experience for everyone involved.

Thank you for reading the ultimate guide on preparing for a successful Pop-Up Event or Festival! Throughout this book, we have covered everything you need to know, from answering all your questions about Pop-Up Events and Festivals to providing detailed preparation tips. We have even included a dedicated chapter with a handy checklist to ensure your events are flawlessly planned. With the insights and strategies shared, you're now ready to embark on a journey to create truly memorable Pop-Up Event or Festival experiences. Whether you are a seasoned event planner or a first-timer, this guide equips you with the tools and knowledge to ensure your event is a resounding success.

Yours Truly,
(Ms.Unexpected) Tameka and (DJ Mojo) Jordan Crews